SCHOLASTIC

READ & RESPOND

Helping children discover the pleasure and power of reading

FOR AGES 9–11

Published in the UK by Scholastic, 2023

Scholastic Distribution Centre, Bosworth Avenue, Tournament Fields, Warwick, CV34 6UQ

Scholastic Ireland, 89E Lagan Road, Dublin Industrial Estate, Glasnevin, Dublin, D11 HP5F

SCHOLASTIC and associated logos are trademarks and/or registered trademarks of Scholastic Inc.

www.scholastic.co.uk

© 2023 Scholastic Limited

1 2 3 4 5 6 7 8 9 3 4 5 6 7 8 9 0 1 2

A CIP catalogue record for this book is available from the British Library.
ISBN 978-0702-31951-8

Printed and bound by Ashford Colour Press
The book is made of materials from well-managed,
FSC®-certified forests and other controlled sources.

Extracts from *The National Curriculum in England, English Programme of Study* © Crown Copyright. Reproduced under the terms of the Open Government Licence (OGL). http://www.nationalarchives.gov.uk/doc/open-government-licence/version/3

Authors Sally Burt and Debbie Ridgard
Editorial team Rachel Morgan, Vicki Yates, Caroline Low, Liz Evans
Series designer Andrea Lewis
Typesetter QBS Learning
Illustrator Andy Rowland/Advocate Art Ltd

Acknowledgements
The publishers gratefully acknowledge permission to reproduce the following material:
Scholastic Children's Books for the use of the text extracts and cover from *Brightstorm: A Sky-ship Adventure* written by Vashti Hardy.

Every effort has been made to trace copyright holders for the works reproduced in this book, and the publishers apologise for any inadvertent omissions.

For supporting online resources go to:
www.scholastic.co.uk/read-and-respond/books/brightstorm/online-resources
Access key: Explain

CONTENTS

How to use Read & Respond in your classroom...   4

Curriculum links   6

Guided reading   9

Shared reading   13

Grammar, punctuation & spelling   19

Plot, character & setting   25

Talk about it   32

Get writing   38

Assessment   44

How to use Read & Respond in your classroom...

Read & Respond provides teaching ideas related to a specific well-loved children's book. Each Read & Respond book is divided into the following sections:

ABOUT THE BOOK AND AUTHOR

Gives you some background information about the book and the author.

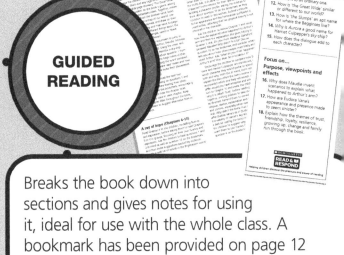

GUIDED READING

Breaks the book down into sections and gives notes for using it, ideal for use with the whole class. A bookmark has been provided on page 12 containing **comprehension** questions. The children can be directed to refer to these as they read. Find comprehensive guided reading sessions on the supporting online resources.

SHARED READING

Provides extracts from the children's book with associated notes for focused work. There is also one non-fiction extract that relates to the children's book.

GRAMMAR, PUNCTUATION & SPELLING

Provides word-level work related to the children's book so you can teach grammar, punctuation, spelling and **vocabulary** in context.

PLOT, CHARACTER & SETTING

Contains activity ideas focused on the plot, characters and the setting of the story.

TALK ABOUT IT

Oracy, **fluency**, and speaking and listening activities. These activities may be based directly on the children's book or be broadly based on the themes and concepts of the story.

GET WRITING

Provides writing activities related to the children's book. These activities may be based directly on the children's book or be broadly based on the themes and concepts of the story.

ASSESSMENT

Contains short activities that will help you assess whether the children have understood concepts and curriculum objectives. They are designed to be informal activities to feed into your planning.

SUPPORTING ONLINE RESOURCE

Online you can find a host of supporting documents including planning information, comprehensive guided reading sessions and guidance on teaching reading.

www.scholastic.co.uk/read-and-respond/books/brightstorm/online-resources
Access key: Explain

Help children develop a love of reading for pleasure.

Activities

The activities follow the same format:

- **Objective:** the objective for the lesson. It will be based upon a curriculum objective, but will often be more specific to the focus being covered.

- **What you need:** a list of resources you need to teach the lesson, including photocopiable pages.

- **What to do:** the activity notes.

- **Differentiation:** this is provided where specific and useful differentiation advice can be given to support and/or extend the learning in the activity. Differentiation by providing additional adult support has not been included as this will be at a teacher's discretion based upon specific children's needs and ability, as well as the availability of support.

The activities are numbered for reference within each section and should move through the text sequentially – so you can use the lesson while you are reading the book. Once you have read the book, most of the activities can be used in any order you wish.

CURRICULUM LINKS

Section	Activity	Curriculum objectives
Guided reading		Comprehension: To maintain positive attitudes to reading and understanding of what they read.
Shared reading	1	Comprehension: To identify how language, structure and presentation contribute to meaning.
	2	Comprehension: To discuss and evaluate how authors use language, including figurative language, considering the impact on the reader.
	3	Comprehension: To identify how language, structure and presentation contribute to meaning.
	4	Comprehension: To summarise the main ideas drawn from more than one paragraph, identifying key details that support the main ideas.
Grammar, punctuation and spelling	1	Vocabulary, grammar and punctuation: To use brackets, dashes or commas to indicate parenthesis.
	2	Spelling: To use the first three or four letters of a word to check spelling, meaning or both of these in a dictionary.
	3	Vocabulary, grammar and punctuation: To use hyphens to avoid ambiguity.
	4	Vocabulary, grammar and punctuation: To use the perfect form of verbs to mark relationships of time and cause.
	5	Vocabulary, grammar and punctuation: To use expanded noun phrases to convey complicated information concisely.
	6	Comprehension: To check that the text makes sense to them, discussing their understanding and explaining the meaning of words in context.
Plot, character and setting	1	Comprehension: To make comparisons within and across books.
	2	Comprehension: To discuss and evaluate how authors use language, including figurative language, considering the impact on the reader.
	3	Comprehension: To summarise the main ideas drawn from more than one paragraph, identifying key details that support the main ideas.
	4	Comprehension: To discuss and evaluate how authors use language, including figurative language, considering the impact on the reader.
	5	Comprehension: To draw inferences such as inferring characters' feelings, thoughts and motives from their actions, and justifying inferences with evidence.
	6	Comprehension: To draw inferences such as inferring characters' feelings, thoughts and motives from their actions, and justifying inferences with evidence.
	7	Comprehension: To identify and discuss themes and conventions in and across a wide range of writing.
	8	Comprehension: To identify and discuss themes and conventions in and across a wide range of writing.

Section	Activity	Curriculum objectives
Talk about it	1	Spoken language: To use relevant strategies to build their vocabulary.
	2	Spoken language: To participate in discussions, presentations, performances, role play, improvisations and debates.
	3	Spoken language: To select and use appropriate registers for effective communication; to articulate and justify opinions.
	4	Spoken language: To speak audibly and fluently with an increasing command of Standard English.
	5	Spoken language: To maintain attention and participate actively in collaborative conversations, staying on topic and initiating and responding to comments.
	6	Spoken language: To consider and evaluate different viewpoints, attending to and building on the contributions of others.
Get writing	1	Composition: To note and develop initial ideas, drawing on reading and research where necessary; to use further organisational and presentational devices to structure text and to guide the reader.
	2	Composition: To note and develop initial ideas.
	3	Composition: To identify the audience for and purpose of the writing; to proofread for spelling and punctuation errors.
	4	Composition: To use further organisational and presentational devices to structure text and to guide the reader; to ensure the consistent and correct use of tense throughout a piece of writing; to ensure correct subject and verb agreement.
	5	Composition: To select appropriate grammar and vocabulary, understanding how such choices can change and enhance meaning. In narratives, to describe settings, characters and atmosphere.
	6	Composition: To use further organisational and presentational devices to structure text and to guide the reader; to use a wide range of devices to build cohesion; to proofread for spelling and punctuation errors.
Assessment	1	Composition: In narratives, to describe settings, characters and atmosphere and integrate dialogue to convey character and advance the action.
	2	Comprehension: To understand what they read in books they can read independently by asking questions to improve their understanding of a text.
	3	Composition: To distinguish between the language of speech and writing and choose the appropriate register; to proofread for spelling and punctuation errors.
	4	Spoken language: To gain, maintain and monitor the interest of the listener(s); to speak audibly and fluently with an increasing command of Standard English.
	5	Composition: To write narratives, considering how authors have developed characters and settings in what pupils have read, listened to or seen performed; to predict what might happen from details stated and implied.
	6	Composition: To précis longer passages; to identify the audience for and purpose of the writing, selecting the appropriate form and using other similar writing as models for their own.

Key facts

◉ **Title:**
Brightstorm: A Sky-Ship Adventure

◉ **Author:**
Vashti Hardy

◉ **First published:**
2018 by Scholastic Children's Books

◉ **Awards:**
Shortlisted for the Waterstones Children's Book Prize 2019
The Bookseller Association's Children's Book of the Season – Spring 2018
Shortlisted for the Books Are My Bag Readers Awards 2018
Longlisted for the Blue Peter Book Awards
West Sussex Children's Story Book Award 2019 Winner

◉ **Did you know?**
Vashti Hardy was influenced by the real-life explorer Ernest Shackleton when coming up with the idea for *Brightstorm*.

About the book

Brightstorm, the first in the series of Sky-ship Adventures, is a fantasy adventure about a race to reach the icy South Polaris in the far reaches of the Third Continent. The Brightstorm twins, Arthur and Maudie, come from a family of explorers. When they learn of the mysterious events and disappearance of their father on his most recent expedition, they decide to seek out the truth. Joining a group of explorers on the sky-ship *Aurora*, they set off – not only to win the race but also to solve the mystery of their father's disappearance and restore their family name. Their rival, Eudora Vane, from a highly respected explorer family, will seemingly stop at nothing to win at all costs – or is there more to it? The twins are determined and brave, and with the support of the crew, a few vital tools and scientific solutions, they prove a match for Eudora as they expose lies and uncover secrets hidden in the snow. The twins discover more than the truth; they experience the value of family, trust, friendship, integrity and resilience in the face of failure. This action-packed story takes the reader into a fantasy, archaic world of sky-ships, distant lands, explorers and intelligent beasts.

About the author

Vashti Hardy is an award-winning children's book author. Her stories appeal to children of all ages and have been translated into many languages to be read around the world. She has a teaching degree, specialising in English, and a master's degree in Creative Writing from the University of Chichester. She left primary school teaching to become a copywriter and digital marketing executive and to focus on her writing. She loves writing fantasy for children because they are so open to imagining things – she believes imagination can take you anywhere. Having loved real-life explorers and inventors from history, she always wanted to write a story about explorers. Once her ideas came together, it took about a year to write *Brightstorm*, the first in the Sky-ship Adventure series. *Darkwhispers* and *Firesong* are the sequels to *Brightstorm*; her other books include *Wildspark* and *The Griffin Gate*.

Her favourite book as a child was *Rebecca's World* by Terry Nation because it opened her eyes to the world of adventure and fantasy and made her want to be a writer.

'I love tales of exploring and fantasy adventure and have always been fascinated by real-life adventurers from history such as Ernest Shackleton and Amelia Earhart. I love to get out and about in nature whenever I can, but I must admit my favourite exploring and adventuring takes place in my imagination.'

GUIDED READING ▶

Disaster (Chapters 1–3)

Encourage the children to explore the cover – illustrations, blurb and any taglines or reviews, as well as the inside page showing 'The Great Wide' map. Invite discussion on the book's genre, asking for evidence to substantiate ideas. Together, review the map and elicit from the children what looks familiar or different to a map of our world. Use question 12 on the bookmark and draw on their knowledge of geography and map work to begin a running list of similar/different things about the world in the novel (for example, world is 'Great Wide'; has continents but fewer).

Read Chapter 1, inviting volunteers to jump in as the different characters (Arthur, Maudie, Mistress Poacher, Madame Gainsford). Using the cover and Chapter 1, invite learners to describe a sky-ship and how it might work. Introduce question 1 from the bookmark and discuss the tragic news of their father's apparent death, noting the word 'perished'. Ask: *What do 'Her words were lead' mean and how does it suggest the way the twins feel?* (devastated, crushed by a great weight)

Invite the children to read the next two chapters in groups, focusing on questions 1 and 2 on the bookmark before sharing their ideas. Refer to question 7 on the bookmark, encouraging the children to notice how the chapter titles summarise the key issue in each chapter. Keep track of the chapter titles throughout the book, inviting volunteers to suggest alternative titles or predict events.

A ray of hope (Chapters 4–10)

Read Chapter 4 to the children, modelling fluency and expression, before asking them to read Chapters 5 to 9 in groups, focusing on their own fluency and expression. Ask the children to bear questions 1 and 2 in mind as well as question 13 on the bookmark and then invite suggestions backed by evidence. Create a wall list of words in the Brightstorm world and their equivalents in our world, for example 'chimes' and 'moon-cycles'. Encourage the children to add words as they encounter them. Together, discuss question 3 on the bookmark, analysing Arthur's reasons for saying, 'It doesn't fit.' Ask: *What does it make them want to do?* (find out the truth) Ask: *Is Eudora Vane a good or bad character?* Invite reasons for their opinions and begin building a character profile, asking the children to think about question 17 on the bookmark as they continue to read. In this section, Eudora's attitude to her appearance and the Pomeranian puffbacks is unattractive, reflecting that her physical beauty is not mirrored in her character.

Ask the children to review Chapter 1 and recall how Maudie explained what happened to Arthur's arm and then the explanation she gives Felicity in Chapter 7. Ask: *Do you think Madame Gainsford believed Maudie? Why didn't Felicity?* Discuss question 16 on the bookmark and consider what it tells you about how often people react badly and upset Arthur. Ask: *What do you think happened to Arthur's arm? And does he mind about it?*

Encourage the children to compare how Eudora Vane and Harriet Culpepper are introduced, asking which character they would prefer to spend time with and why. With this in mind, invite volunteers to explain the two offers the twins receive in Chapter 9 and predict which one they will accept. Ask: *Which offer would you have accepted and why?* Together, turn to Chapter 10 and invite the children to predict why it is called 'Trust', before reading the chapter together, inviting children to take over the reading as directed. Remind them to consider punctuation (ellipses, dashes, exclamation and question marks) and context, especially when reading dialogue. Ask: *Why didn't the twins trust Harriet Culpepper after Eudora Vane's visit?* (Eudora cast doubt on the viability of Harriet's sky-ship.) Finally, ask: *Who is behind locking the twins in the cellar?* Encourage the children to suggest why someone might not want them to join Harriet Culpepper in reference to question 4 on the bookmark.

Life on the *Aurora* (Chapters 11–14)

Read Chapter 11 together, inviting children to jump in as characters in the dialogue, particularly where Arthur and Maudie talk in short sentences, finishing each other's words, after making it onto the sky-ship. The children should then read on in groups to the end of Chapter 13, bearing questions 5 and 14 in mind and making notes about life on the ship with the crew. Ask: *What does Arthur discover about the different explorer families? Do the Culpepper and Vane descriptions match what you know about Harriet and Eudora?* Share answers.

Read Chapter 14 together, considering question 15 on the bookmark. Encourage the children to focus on the dialogue and explain what they enjoy about it, for example, the authenticity and humour, the puns ('riveting', 'up to speed') and Felicity's unusual expressions, linking it to their knowledge of informal language being characteristic of dialogue over narrative. Ask the children to reflect on why Harriet gives Arthur the explorer's journal and to predict whether it will become important in the story.

Desert Sands to Great Glacies (Chapters 15–18)

Read on with the children, focusing on the different landscapes, noting geographical features, weather and animal life. Encourage groups to identify similar landscapes on a physical map of the world and to research the dangers of quicksand and how best to escape from it. Ask: *What does the bag of silver First Continent coins found on the bandit suggest?* (bribe to attack the *Aurora*) Discuss question 11 on the bookmark in relation to Altan and Parthena. Ask: *What other sapients have appeared in the book?* (Miptera, Madame Gainsford's stoat and Queenie)

Batzorig wonders whether other explorer families have been bought off or sabotaged after Harriet explains what has been going on and why she kept her technology and ship secret. Ask: *What do you think and why?* (clues: kidnapping, Eudora's offer, the *Fontaine*, the *Fire-Bird*, bandits) *What confirms the twins' suspicions about Eudora Vane?* (hidden writing in lemon juice) *What did Arthur think he'd seen at the end of Chapter 18?* (Miptera) *Does that bode well or badly for the* Aurora? *Why?*

The case against Eudora (Chapters 19–23)

Read Chapter 19 together, again modelling fluency and expression, inviting the children to jump in as you go through. Ask: *What clues suggest the explosion was not accidental?* (gnaw marks, silver insect) *What else implies Eudora Vane is behind the disaster?* (broke Explorer's Code; insurance man on her ship) Discuss question 6 on the bookmark, recalling earlier details as well as the evidence here.

Discuss how Maudie told Arthur he wasn't thinking when he rushed off into the forest, but he couldn't stop himself. Ask: *What does he want to know so much that he puts everyone in danger?* (the truth) *How does Harriet reassure him?* (plan to go to South Polaris with twins) Find out if any of the children have had a similar experience to Arthur – wanting something so much that they don't think about the consequences.

Recap the end of Chapter 19 and begin discussing question 9 on the bookmark. Ask: *Which challenge is more important to the twins – finding out about Dad or the South Polaris expedition?* Ask the children to keep a mental note as they read, considering what the twins might do if the challenges come into conflict.

Read to the end of Chapter 20 together, noting how the author uses italics to express words in thoughts rather than ordinary dialogue. Ask: *Do you agree with Harriet that the twins understand the thought-wolves because they're younger with more open minds?* Encourage everyday examples where children sometimes find things easier to imagine or understand than adults. Ask the children to read on in groups, collecting clues about what happened to the *Violetta*'s crew. At the end, invite them to explain what they think happened on the first trip and how it differs from Eudora Vane's version to the Geographical Society (13 graves, 14 places set, everyone left suddenly, bitter smell of poison, empty fuel stores, Dad's allergy to eggs – and what the thought-wolves told Arthur) Ask: *Is it a good idea for Arthur and Maudie to go to the* Victorious? *What proof might they find?*

The plan (Chapters 23–28)

Ask the children to read Chapter 23 individually before sharing the evidence the twins found. Then ask them to predict why Eudora Vane has a similar locket to Dad's with 'VE' (not 'EV') engraved on it. Read on to the end of Chapter 25, focusing on how Arthur still acts before thinking, without regard for others. Ask: *Why was Harriet angry with the twins? Was she right to be angry?* (yes – they put the crew in danger) Encourage the children to recall Chapter 10 'Trust' and what Welby said to the twins, and to then consider question 9 again on the bookmark. Ask: *What do you think Arthur and Maudie have learned after their experience on the* Victorious? Discuss the twins – how they feel about each other and how they feel about the expedition. Ask: *Do they both want the same things?* (not entirely) Encourage reasoned answers, focusing on their different characters and abilities. Ask: *How do they solve the problem of Arthur losing the compass?* (Arthur's iron arm that Maudie had magnetised)

Read Chapters 26 to 27 asking children to jump in and take over the reading. Praise reading with fluency and expression and, where necessary, re-read sections to allow different groups to practise and improve. Invite the children to share their knowledge about stalagmites and stalactites; if possible, show images sourced from the internet or books to support their visualisation. When Parthena goes to Maudie after reading their father's diary, Arthur realises she needs Parthena's comfort more than he does. Discuss why this might be and what it says about Arthur that he recognises this. Then talk about what the team see as they exit the cave; Harriet calls it the 'southern aurora'. Share pictures and images of the Aurora Borealis/Aurora Polaris and make a further link between the Brightstorm world and the world we live in. Explain to the children that in Greek and Roman mythology, Aurora was the goddess of the dawn, then discuss question 14 on the bookmark again, encouraging both literal and figurative links.

Read Chapter 28 together, focusing on the build-up to the final climax. Ask: *What tipped Maudie over the edge making her race towards the* Victorious? (She realised Eudora Vane wanted to discredit Dad, and wanted to know why.) Together, discuss the climax and revelation that Eudora was their mother's younger sister, recalling the clues (locket with 'VE', long history and pride of Vanes as an exploring family, Ernest Brightstorm being first explorer in his family). Discuss prejudice and how it's often fuelled by things that really don't matter, for example being an explorer should have been enough to gain respect; it shouldn't matter that Ernest Brightstorm wasn't part of a traditional explorer family. Point out that Harriet knew the twins' heritage before inviting them to join her expedition; she was interested in them as individuals, not their family history, although she understood their pride and desire to clear their name – a totally different attitude to Eudora's.

Goodbye? (Chapters 29–31)

Read the remaining chapters together and review the book's structure in light of question 8 on the bookmark, from the introduction, problem/challenge and build-up through to the climax and the resolution, then discuss question 10 on the bookmark. Turn to the front cover and ask: *What supports this book being the first in a series?* (tagline: 'A Sky-ship Adventure'). Invite opinions about whether the children enjoyed the story and whether they would read a further adventure with the same characters and setting, especially with their enemy, Eudora Vane, still at large.

At the end of the book, discuss question 18 on the bookmark, inviting evidence to support the different themes. Then survey the children to find out if they noticed any other themes underlying the story, for example, environmentalism, unique but differing abilities and not wanting to use guns. End by asking if they agree with Ernest Brightstorm's words to Arty: *'Fear kills more dreams than failure ever will. You can be comfortable or courageous – never both at once.'* Encourage reasons relating to the different characters and their own lives.

Brightstorm
by Vashti Hardy

Focus on...
Meaning

1. How do Arthur and Maudie's circumstances change?
2. Give examples that demonstrate Arthur and Maudie's special relationship as twins.
3. Why does the locket that Parthena brings cast doubt on what happened to Ernest Brightstorm?
4. What is the Polaris Challenge and why is it so important?
5. What advantage does the *Aurora* have and how does it help the expedition?
6. What reveals that Eudora doesn't have the true explorer spirit?

Focus on...
Organisation

7. Explain the purpose of the chapters having titles as well as numbers.
8. How do Dad's words 'Don't call it a dream, call it a plan' guide the children and the storyline?
9. What is Arthur and Maudie's main aim? When does their aim conflict with that of the *Aurora*?
10. How does the ending suggest that the book is the first in a series or may have a sequel?

Brightstorm
by Vashti Hardy

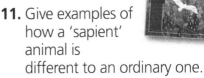

Focus on...
Language and features

11. Give examples of how a 'sapient' animal is different to an ordinary one.
12. How is 'the Great Wide' similar or different to our world?
13. How is 'the Slumps' an apt name for where the Begginses live?
14. Why is *Aurora* a good name for Harriet Culpepper's sky-ship?
15. How does the dialogue add to each character?

Focus on...
Purpose, viewpoints and effects

16. Why does Maudie invent scenarios to explain what happened to Arthur's arm?
17. How are Eudora Vane's appearance and presence made to seem sinister?
18. Explain how the themes of trust, friendship, loyalty, resilience, growing up, change and family run through the book.

SHARED READING ▶

Extract 1

- Read Extract 1 and ask the children to summarise what is happening. Ask: *Is this an exciting or intriguing start to a novel? What questions do you have about the setting and characters after reading it?*

- Invite volunteers to identify unfamiliar words ('Lontown', 'chime', 'uniscope') and give a more familiar meaning/alternative. Explain that other words may be unfamiliar because they are technical jargon ('haltway fans', 'swivel blade propellor').

- Circle 'engrossed', 'juddered' and 'straddled'. Explain each word in everyday language using the downloadable Focus word table from the supporting online resources (see page 5). Provide definitions for other words the children may find tricky (for example, 'rumbled', 'launch', 'ridge'), also using everyday language.

- Underline 'engrossed' in '…if you hadn't been so engrossed in *Volcanic Islands of the North*…' Ask: *What does this tell you about how Arty reads books?* (gets totally absorbed) *Why is an ellipsis used?* (Maudie didn't need to say that Arthur didn't notice the time as they both get the point.)

- Read out 'But as he tried to pull himself up, it juddered and slipped down.' Ask: *What are the difficulties for Arthur's metal arm compared to a real arm?* (grip is difficult on a slippery surface) Invite the children to describe the movement and sound 'juddered' implies and to suggest synonyms.

- Review the powerful verbs in the extract. In groups, ask children to re-read it, underlining interesting verbs noting how they add detail – for example, sound or movement ('rumbled', 'juddered', 'launch', 'grabbed', 'swung', 'hooked', 'heaved', 'scrambled', 'straddled'). Discuss how a thesaurus helps the children to choose powerful verbs in their writing.

- Organise groups to re-read the extract, focusing on fluency and expression to enhance the sense of drama and the understanding between Arthur and Maudie.

Extract 2

- Organise the children in pairs to read the extract focusing on how the author creates drama and visual impact. In their first reading, encourage them to visualise the scene by drawing a plan of the sky-ship, showing where everything and everyone is, including the other sky-ships and the ground below.

- Invite volunteers to share experiences of flying, for example when going on holiday, and to describe the ground looking down from above. Ask: *What simile in the extract describes the city below?* ('like a child's wooden model') Invite alternative similes to describe the effect.

- Briefly revise the difference between similes and metaphors and then ask pairs to underline examples in the passage. Ask: *Why do authors use figurative language?* (Using different senses and unusual imagery increases impact.) Survey the class for their favourite simile or metaphor in the extract and invite pairs to come up with their own similes or metaphors to describe the scene. Praise creativity.

- Now focus on powerful, descriptive words (for example, 'rising powerfully', 'wings spread majestically wide', 'dwarfed in size', 'hair and scarf flowing messily in the wind', 'deadlier than a glue bog') and invite the children to discuss their impact. Ask: *Have you ever felt a 'fizzling knot of competitiveness', or any other feeling, forming inside you?* Share experiences and feelings and their physical impact, for example before a race on sports day or arriving somewhere new.

- Now ask the children to read the extract aloud in groups of five, using their enhanced appreciation of the text to bring the scene to life, using expression, gestures and body language to support the characters' words and context.

Extract 3

- Read Extract 3 to the children modelling fluency and expression. Together analyse different aspects of the reading and how you approached them: short or single-line paragraphs, dialogue, dash, ellipses at end of dialogue and in middle, twins finishing each other's sentences, ending on a single-word sentence. Ask the children to annotate their copies using underlining, notes and colours to remind them how to approach the reading.

- Use questions to stimulate discussion and assess comprehension as you work through. Ask: *Why do the twins finish each other's sentences?* (They think the same thoughts, having shared the same experiences; they are very close, which is common in twins, especially with their mother being dead and their father often away before he died.)

- Ask: *Why is it important that Harriet and Felicity have been like family?* (no family of their own) *What does it tell us about families?* (they are all different; family is more about loving, trusting and supporting each other than being related)

- Consider the solemnity of the moment. Ask: *Why did Harriet and Felicity leave the twins in the ice cave?* (to give them privacy to say goodbye to their father in their own way) *Why was it important to say goodbye?* (to give closure to that part of their lives and allow them to look forward) *How do you think the children were feeling?* (Discuss a range of emotions from sad to proud, optimistic and even happy.) *Were they talking fast or slowly?* (a mixture: fast in parts but reflectively towards the end)

- Now ask the children to read the extract in groups of three, using their notes and deeper understanding to bring the passage to life, especially the dialogue. Allow time for practice.

Extract 4

- Hand out enlarged copies of Extract 4. In pairs, invite the children to skim the text and identify the features (headings, timeline, dates, facts, bullets, diagram with labels, glossary) and the text type (formal, factual, historical). Ask: *How do the features guide the reader? How is a non-fiction text different to a fiction text? What is a fact?* (something that can be proved true) *Can a fiction text contain facts?* (yes)

- In pairs, invite the children to read aloud, taking turns to read a sentence each to develop fluency. They then use coloured pens to highlight the key words: the most important nouns, verbs and adjectives relating to the topic.

- Then, ask the children to identify five important facts in the text. Come together and share ideas and discuss which facts are the most important in terms of the title. Ask: *What is the main idea of the text? What information do you think follows this timeline of events?*

- Move on to identify and explain topic-specific words such as 'free flight' (not tied or held to the ground), 'sphere' (a round shape), 'miles per hour' (distance covered in an hour).

- Explore focus words from the text such as 'manned', 'steer' and 'enabled'. Use the focus-word table from the supporting online resources (see page 5) to provide everyday explanations, find dictionary definitions and then encourage children to use the words in different contexts by writing sentences.

- Individually, ask children to use the information provided to draw and label a picture of the very first hot air balloon with its unusual passengers. Include a heading and a glossary.

Extract 1

The heavy chug of the sky-ship firing its engines rumbled through Lontown.

"Quick, pull me up!" Arthur called from the lower roof.

"Clamp your hand onto the pipe – see if it's strong enough to take your weight," said Maudie.

"We're going to miss it, Maud!"

"We're not, it's only just fired up, and if you hadn't been so engrossed in *Volcanic Islands of the North*…"

"If you hadn't insisted on adjusting my arm…"

"So, we both lost track of the chime. Come on, Arty, I want to see if the modification to the fingers helped."

Arthur sighed. Using his left hand he raised the iron arm attached to his right shoulder, then folded the metal fingers around the pipe. But as he tried to pull himself up, it juddered and slipped down.

Maudie shook her head and looked away in thought. "They need more tension."

"Just help me up, will you?"

"Perhaps if I use Harris screws," she said.

Arthur found a small jut of brick about halfway up the wall between upper and lower roof, and used it to launch himself with his left foot. He narrowly grabbed the lip of the roof and swung his other leg so that his foot hooked the edge, then he heaved his body up. "Thanks for nothing, Maud."

"You totally had it, Arty."

Their eyes met. "Race you to the top!" they said together, then scrambled up the tiles like a pair of wild cats.

They reached the topmost part of the roof at the same time and straddled the ridge, out of breath and laughing.

"Poacher will freak if she catches us up here again," Maudie said.

"It won't be the first time."

"Or the last."

At that moment, the sky-ship rose from the distant docks above the domes and spires of the city skyline. Maudie took her uniscope from her tool belt. "Standard double engine… Ooh, dipped haltway fans and a swivel blade propeller – good choice."

Extract 2

The *Victorious* was visible above the docks a short distance away, rising powerfully into the sky, its wings spread majestically wide. Another sky-ship rose beside it, dwarfed in size. Then another caught Arthur's eye further west. A fizzling knot of competitiveness formed inside him.

"Turn! Turn!" Welby shouted rhythmically from the other side.

Arthur threw all his energy into turning the cog. The great fabric balloon grew bigger by the second and a judder came from the engines below as something fitted into place. Then a repeating *whirr*, *clunk* sounded like a great heartbeat.

Harriet Culpepper stood at the wheel, her hair and scarf flowing messily in the wind. She looked ahead through her binoscope. "Good work," she called. "Get those sails fully open – we need more lift, to aid the balloon."

Great connected cogs with handles ran along the inner edges of the deck. Half of the crew lined each side. Maudie took the handle in front.

The sun, due east of the city, was a glowing peach rising over the ridge. Below, the houses and streets had become miniature, like a child's wooden model.

"Move the cogs or we'll end up crashing into one of those towers and it'll be the shortest expedition in history!" Harriet ordered from the central wheel.

"Put your backs into it," Welby called from the other side.

Felicity patted Arthur on the shoulder. "Focus on the cog – it's just like stirring Granny's stottle cake – that mixture was deadlier than a glue bog. C'mon Arthur, we can do this. You just swung one-armed from a flying house; anything's possible!"

"Come on, port side – push harder," Arthur shouted along the crew line.

Behind him, Maudie was encouraging the other half to turn faster. The cogs gained momentum, then there was movement and a flash of white to the sides. Great sails began extending from the *Aurora* into view of the deck. It was beautiful, like the wings of a bird unfolding for their first flight.

Extract 3

When they felt ready to embark on the journey back, Arthur and Maudie visited the ice cave where their father lay…

"Dad, we didn't understand what you were trying to tell us by sending Parthena with the locket, but we know now," said Arthur. "We came, for you, and we made it all the way to South Polaris."

"It wasn't quite as we'd hoped it would be, I'm afraid," Maudie said.

"There won't be any reward and we'll have to find a way to make our own way in Lontown…"

"But we know we can do it…"

Arthur looked sideways at Maudie and smiled.

"Because we did what we came to do – we found the truth."

"And we did lots of cool stuff on the way…"

"We crossed the Second Continent and…"

"We met kings, and we even crossed…"

"The biggest ocean on the planet…"

"Only to survive…"

"Sabotage."

"We'll let you guess who was behind that."

"And we crashed, over the Everlasting Forest…"

"But every crew member lived."

"We met the thought-wolves…"

"And found out how to be friends with them."

"They saved us!"

"Parthena was amazing."

"And all the way, Harrie and Felicity…"

They both fell silent for a moment.

"They've been beside us every step," Maudie began

"I mean they've really been there for us…"

"Like…family."

The twins looked at each other and smiled.

"We're going to be fine, Dad," said Maudie. "And we're going to make you proud, even if we have no evidence left to prove what Eudora Vane did, we're going to rebuild the Brightstorm name. Somehow."

Extract 4

The invention of hot air balloons and airships

Before aeroplanes, early inventors tried various ways to get humans to fly.

1783: In France, in front of a large crowd, the first humans went up in a hot air balloon invented by the Montgolfier brothers – the first manned free flight in history. Within a couple of years, a hot air balloon flew across the English Channel in the first long-distance flight.

1852: Henri Giffard, a French engineer, attached a small, steam-powered engine to a propeller, which enabled the first airship to travel for 17 miles (approximately 27km) at five miles per hour (approximately 8km/h). This was the first powered **LTA craft**.

1896: Gasoline-powered airships were invented, which were faster and more powerful and more harmful to the environment.

Did you know? *Initially, hot air balloons were flown by heating the air inside the balloon while still on the ground or using an on-board fire. Later, hot air balloons carried their own fuel using burners to re-heat the air inside the balloon. As inventors improved the designs, balloons were able to fly longer and further, but they remained hard to steer. Attempts were made to improve this by changing the balloon's shape from a sphere to an egg-shape.*

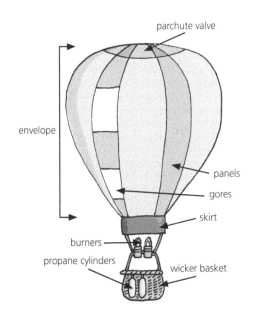

Fast facts:
- A sheep, a duck and a rooster were the first passengers onboard a hot air balloon in 1783.
- The first letter delivered via airmail was carried from Dover to Calais in January 1785.
- A hot air balloon is an unpowered LTA craft and an airship is a powered LTA craft.

Glossary:
LTA craft lighter-than-air craft

GRAMMAR, PUNCTUATION & SPELLING ▶

1. A dash to add a little extra

Objective
To use dashes to mark parenthesis.

What you need
Copies of *Brightstorm*.

What to do

- Revise hyphens and dashes. Ask the children to identify the hyphen and dash in the final paragraph of Extract 1. Ask: *How are they different?* (hyphens: short, no space either side; dashes: longer and spaced) Ask: *What does the hyphen do here?* (joins two words to form a compound noun) *What does the dash do here?* (adds an afterthought to Maudie's sentence)

- Explain that dashes have several grammatical roles, one of which is parenthesis. Parenthesis is a word, phrase or clause added to a sentence to provide extra or clarifying information. When a parenthesis is removed, the sentence must still make sense on its own. Parenthesis can be marked by brackets, commas or dashes. Dashes can therefore be used to add information, either in pairs (middle of sentence) or singly (beginning/end of sentence), often as a preceding or afterthought, especially in dialogue.

- Organise groups to find examples of dashes in Chapter 1, identifying the main sentence and the additional information. Now ask groups to find further examples in a chapter of their choice, noting page numbers and identifying how they are used – whether in pairs or singly. Hold a plenary session to review the examples.

Differentiation
Support: Specify a chapter for children to search (for example, Chapters 5, 9, 13 or 16).

Extension: Ask children to explore dashes at the end of dialogue, for example in Chapters 8, 9 or 17, and then explain their role to the class.

2. Dictionary delve

Objective
To use the first three or four letters of a word to check spelling and meaning.

What you need
Dictionaries, photocopiable page 22 'Dictionary delve'.

What to do

- Revise using a dictionary, focus on words with the same initial letters. Write these words on the board: 'bridge, bribery, brigand, briskly, brilliance'. Invite a volunteer to explain how to look up a word in a dictionary (look at the initial letter of word to locate it in dictionary, then the second, and so on). Children can look up any unfamiliar words and share them with the class, noting which words appear just before and after their target words.

- Now ask the children to write the words in alphabetical order. Pairs can compare lists to check for differences before swapping and checking their order using a dictionary. Ask: *What do you do if the fourth letter is also the same?* (look at next letter)

- Write more word groups on the board with the same first three letters, for example: 'professor, prospect, promise, pronunciation, provide'; 'champion, character, chapter, chalk, chamber' (discuss difference in pronunciation of the first three letters); 'adventure, advantage, adversary, advertise, adverb'. Add more words of your own and then ask the children to complete photocopiable page 22 'Dictionary delve'.

Differentiation
Support: Give children a list of words with only the first two letters being the same.

Extension: Pairs can create their own lists to challenge each other.

3. Hyphen work

Objective
To use hyphens to avoid ambiguity.

What you need
Copies of *Brightstorm*.

What to do

- Use Chapter 1 to differentiate between dashes (longer, space either side) and hyphens (shorter, no space either side), writing 'sky-ship', 'moon-cycle' and 'far-off (lands)' on the board. Ask: *What is the hyphen's role in these words?* (creates compound words) *What word class are the hyphenated/compound words?* (noun, noun, adjective) Explore the word classes of the root words, noting how the word class can change in the compound word, for example 'twelve-year-old twins'.

- Explain that compound words are sometimes joined by hyphens (as above) but sometimes they are written as a single word (for example, broomstick). Invite suggestions for both hyphenated and single-word compounds and write them on the board, noting the word classes of the root words compared to the compounds.

- Keep a running wall display of interesting compound words in *Brightstorm*, for example 'monkey-crawl', 'good-for-nothing', 'whirr-clunk' and the invented 'Wide' words ('sky-ship', 'moon-cycle', 'moon-bright', 'star-speckled', 'two-legs', 'thought-wolves', 'hydra-pump', 'hydra-converter').

- Explain that hyphenating words helps avoid ambiguity and promotes rapid understanding. Write 'stained glass windows' and 'rose covered vines' on the board (Chapter 7) and invite a volunteer to explain the ambiguity and how using a hyphen clarifies meaning ('stained-glass', 'rose-covered'). Point out that many numbers between 20 and 100 have hyphens when written as words (twenty-one), as do fractions (two-thirds) and compass directions (north-west) to avoid confusion.

Differentiation

Support: Make root word and hyphen cards to allow children to practise creating compound words.

Extension: Children can explore using hyphens for words with prefixes ending in the same letter as the root word (for example, co-, co-operate) to assist with pronunciation, and then other prefixes that take a hyphen, for example non-, ex-, low-.

4. It's perfect

Objective
To use the perfect form of verbs to mark relationships of time.

What you need
Copies of *Brightstorm*, photocopiable page 23 'It's perfect'.

What to do

- Revise different perfect tenses with the children, explaining that perfect tenses link a past event to another point in time – past, present or future:

  - Present perfect indicates a past action with no specified time, for example 'Felicity <u>has invented</u> a new recipe'.

  - Past perfect indicates an event that happened before a later event in the past, for example 'Arthur <u>had finished</u> his chores when he saw a flash of silver.'

  - Future perfect indicates an event that will have happened by a specified future time, for example 'By their next birthday, Maudie <u>will have fixed</u> Arthur's iron arm.'

- Write the examples on the board, underlining the verbs – both the auxiliary (had, has/have, will have) and the main verb's past participle. Invite volunteers to explain how the perfect tenses are formed (the auxiliary verb 'to have' in the present, past or future tense before the main verb's past participle). Point out that in the present perfect, the auxiliary verb must agree with the subject ('has' or 'have'), whereas in the other perfect tenses it is always 'had' or 'will have'. Children can practise by completing photocopiable page 23 'It's perfect'.

- Discuss which perfect tense would be most common in novels like *Brightstorm* (past perfect) and why (it indicates what had already happened when another event took place – simple past). Point out that 'to have' can appear as a contraction, especially in dialogue, for example I've (I have), he'd (he had) and so on.

Differentiation

Support: Children practise orally with sentence starters: I have...; I had... when...; By next week, I will have...

Extension: Pairs choose a chapter to scan for examples of perfect tenses.

5. Tell me more

Objective

To use expanded noun phrases to convey complicated information.

What you need

Copies of *Brightstorm*, photocopiable page 24 'Tell me more'.

What to do

- Revise phrases: recap that these are groups of words without a verb working together as adjectives, adverbs or nouns. Explain that noun phrases tell us more about the head/main noun in a neat, concise way. Demonstrate how to expand a noun phrase. Write up the sentence 'The *Aurora* was a sky-ship'. Ask: *What type of sky-ship was it?* Invite suggestions for adjectives and phrases to describe the sky-ship (head noun). The children can use the front cover for inspiration and the description in Chapter 12 for relevant adjectives or phrases.

- Draw a mind map surrounding 'sky-ship', noting whether words/phrases describe its look, function or sound. Then, using their ideas, model how to expand a noun phrase, for example 'an unusual, whirring, clunking, water-powered sky-ship with a giant balloon above and wings to the side opened by hand-worked cogs along each side.'

- Write a basic word pattern on the board: 'A/The adjective, adjective, adjective noun with (the/a) adjective, noun'. Small groups now invent noun phrases for explorer, marsh cake and Parthena. Point out that determiners form part of the phrase. Encourage the children to add figurative expressions, especially similes (for example, 'like the wings of a bird'). Invite groups to share their best ones.

- Practise turning the noun phrases into sentences, identifying the main verb (expanded noun phrases may include verb participles but not complete verbs) before asking the class to complete photocopiable page 24 'Tell me more'.

Differentiation

Extension: The children can write a descriptive paragraph using at least two expanded noun phrases on sky-ship, marsh cake, explorer and Parthena, including at least one figurative expression.

6. Word work

Objective

To discuss and explore the meaning of words in context.

What you need

Focus word table from Shared reading of Extract 1, dictionaries/thesauruses.

What to do

- Mix up and display copies of the focus words ('engrossed', 'juddered', 'straddled') and their everyday definitions. Ask the children to match the words and definitions.

- Organise the children into groups. Explain that they will take turns to respond to these prompts: *Have you ever been 'engrossed' in anything? Have you ever heard anything 'judder'? Have you ever 'straddled' anything?* Listen to groups working. Choose interesting responses and ask children to share them with the class, reflecting on how the activity helps build understanding of the target words and the different contexts in which they might use them.

- Now ask the children to use the focus words in their own sentences, choosing their favourite to read aloud. Discuss their sentences and the impact of the focus words.

- Broaden the children's understanding of the focus words further by drawing a target on the board with 'engrossed' as the bull's eye in the centre. Invite volunteers to suggest words with similar meanings (allow dictionaries/thesauruses). Start with a couple of your own, for example, 'absorbed', 'captivated', 'gripped', 'riveted' (note 'riveting' appears in Chapter 14 in word play). Ask the children to write each word close or far from the bull's eye based on how close they judge the similar word's meaning to be. Also ask them to suggest contexts when they might use the words.

- Write the target words and the synonyms from the activity on the working wall, reminding children to aim to use them in their written work.

Differentiation

Support: In pairs, ask the children to devise sentences using the focus words.

Extension: Groups can do the synonym/ target activity with the other target words.

Dictionary delve

- Write the words in each box in alphabetical order. Write the number of letters you had to look at in the brackets.

1.

| relevant | reflection | real | reject | recognise | revelation |

_____ (____)

2.

| dizzy | diagnose | ditch | disturb | diminish | difficult |

_____ (____)

3.

| slow | sloth | slouch | slogged | slobber | sloppily |

_____ (____)

4.

| stew | stepped | steak | stern | steeple | stencil |

_____ (____)

5.

| trek | tremble | tread | treacle | tremor | trench |

_____ (____)

- Choose three words from above. Write your word in the middle, with the words that appear before and after it in the dictionary. Write the word's meaning on the line below.

1. _____ _____ _____

_____

2. _____ _____ _____

_____

3. _____ _____ _____

_____

It's perfect

- Answer these 'What have I done?' questions using the present perfect tense of one of the verbs in the box.

hunt	escape	eat	achieve

1. Arthur _____ not _____ marsh cakes before.

2. The twins _____ _____ from the cellar.

3. Although young, Harriet _____ _____ many things.

4. People _____ _____ the great glacies too much.

- Use the past perfect tense of the verb in brackets, before completing the sentences.

1. After they _____ _____ (cross) the Silent Sea,… _____

_____.

2. The *Aurora* _____

until it _____ _____ (land) on the Third Continent.

3. _____ that Ernest Brightstorm

_____ _____ (reach) South Polaris after all.

- Complete these sentences using the future perfect tense.

1. By the summer holidays, I _____

_____.

2. Before his next birthday, Arthur _____

_____.

3. By this time next year, the twins _____

_____.

Tell me more

- Circle the head noun and main verb in each sentence, then underline the expanded noun phrase. Use a coloured pencil to highlight any figurative expressions (similes).

1. The external wall, between the upper and lower roof, with juts of brick halfway up was perfect for climbing.

2. The ribbon held back wild, rusty-brown hair, whipping around like leaves in the wind.

3. Arthur's magnetised iron arm, tipped by jointed fingers and held on by a leather strap, jostled against his side.

4. The majestic walls lined with majestic pillars and gilt-framed maps, and illuminated by chandeliers glittering like twinkling stars, were like nothing they'd ever seen before.

- Create expanded noun phrases following this pattern: *adjective, adjective, (adjective)* **noun with** *adjective, noun.*

1. _____, _____ beast with _____, _____

2. _____, _____ insect with _____, _____

3. _____, _____, _____ hawk with _____ _____

4. _____, _____, _____ cave with _____ _____

- Write sentences using some of the expanded noun phrases above.

_____

_____

_____

_____

_____

_____

_____

_____

PLOT, CHARACTER & SETTING ▶

1. Fantasy setting

Objective
To investigate settings.

What you need
Copies of *Brightstorm*.

Cross-curricular links
Geography, history

What to do

- Discuss the map on the first page of the book with the children, noting what is similar or different to a map of our world (for example, compass points, continents, seas versus names and layout). Ask: *Why do you think the author has chosen to make things similar yet subtly different to our world?*

- Read Chapters 1 and 2 with the children, noting details of setting as you go (for example, 'Lontown', 'South Polaris') and unfamiliar words (for example, 'sky-ship', 'moon-cycle', 'chime', 'pitch'). Ask: *How do Lontown and the Wide seem similar yet different to life today?* (similar: town, houses, explorers, Geographical Society; different: sky-ships, explorer families and bloodlines). Ask: *What setting details so far suggest this is a fantasy story rather than a historical novel?* (sky-ships, sapient animals, different feel)

- Now have a class discussion on whether this book shares similar characteristics to other novels they have read (or seen), especially in the fantasy/adventure genre, based on the setting. Encourage examples to back up ideas, for example Philip Pullman's books: parallel worlds and daemons.

- Organise children into groups to read the next three chapters, scanning for setting characteristics they have been discussing: similar features, differences, fantasy elements, and recording them in a table with page references. At the end, hold a plenary for all children to share their findings.

Differentiation
Support: Children review only one chapter.

Extension: Children track setting characteristics to share with the class.

2. Action writing

Objective
To evaluate how authors use language.

What you need
Copies of *Brightstorm*.

What to do

- Read Chapter 19, from 'Arthur fell asleep quickly' to the end of the section, modelling expression and fluency to emphasise the drama. Invite children to share their initial reactions to the crash. Ask: *How has the author created drama and action? What senses enhance the panic and fear?*

- Check children understand unfamiliar vocabulary (for example, 'brace', 'lurched' 'cacophony', 'engulfed', 'swathe'). Explain words they are unsure of using everyday language, and give examples of how to use the words.

- Organise the class into groups to re-read the section closely to identify writing techniques with examples. For example, Arthur's thoughts and words in his head (italics); Harriet's dialogue setting the scene not narrative; powerful verbs ('scrambled', 'lurched', 'surged', 'tumbled'); evocative words ('grinding grommets' (alliteration), 'bone-wrenching jolt', 'banked sideways', 'cacophony' (onomatopoeia); imagery ('forest was a swathe of white-topped pines'); sounds ('crashing', 'splitting', 'crack', 'juddered'); sights ('everything flew upward', 'flashes of white and darkness rolled past', 'rush of branches').

- Come together to hold a plenary with a spokesperson from each group outlining their close-reading review of techniques. Build a working wall of their examples of powerful, descriptive writing, with excerpts from the text demonstrating identified techniques.

Differentiation
Support: Specify one or two techniques.

Extension: Children scan for further examples of powerful, descriptive writing to share with the class.

PLOT, CHARACTER & SETTING

3. Who am I?

Objective

To summarise ideas on character drawn from more than one paragraph.

What you need

Copies of *Brightstorm*, photocopiable page 29 'Who am I?'.

What to do

- Review the key characters in the story. Ask: *Who are the protagonists?* (Arthur and Maudie) *Who is the antagonist?* (Eudora Vane) *Who are the other important characters?* (Felicity, Harriet) Explain that even minor characters have a role, for example, Welby, the Begginses, Mistress Poacher, Parthena and even Ernest Brightstorm (in absentia), but some have more important roles in the story than others.

- Write 'Harriet' and 'Felicity' on the board and then read Chapters 7 and 8. Invite volunteers to give their first impressions and predict whether they will be good or bad characters and why.

- Analyse the characters in more depth. Invite volunteers to read out the paragraphs where the characters are introduced: Chapter 7: 'There was a scuffling behind…'; Chapter 8: 'A young woman sat at a table…' Ask: *What do you learn about each character?* Record words and phrases on the board to build a mind map, encouraging the children to think about appearance, demeanour, way of speaking, characteristics, personality and actions – pointing out that what characters do and say shows what they are like, so readers infer details rather than being explicitly told things.

- Organise the children into pairs to finish reading both chapters, gathering further information using the questions on photocopiable page 29 'Who am I?' Come together to share ideas and use the discussion as a baseline to track whether the characters remain true to form as you read on. Create a wall chart to track the characters.

Differentiation

Support: Pairs can focus on one or other character.

Extension: Pairs can do a presentation on the characters, based on their worksheet notes.

4. Informal language

Objective

To identify how language contributes to meaning.

What you need

Copies of *Brightstorm*.

What to do

- Re-read where Felicity first appears in Chapter 7 with you as Felicity, a volunteer as narrator and two others as Arthur and Maudie, modelling reading the dialogue with expression suitable for the language and context.

- Then invite comments on Felicity's informal speaking style. Ask: *Why are there apostrophes at the start and end of some words?* (missing letters: h, g) *What effect does this have?* (suggests an accent) *How does she describe the twins?* ('scared bunnies', 'twinnies', 'popples in a pod') *What does 'if you want the best eggs go straight for the goose' mean?* (go direct to source not via a shop) *What jokes does she make?* ('putting your foot in it', 'footloose and fancy-free'/''armless') *What other informal features characterise her speaking?* (contractions, invented/dialect words ('ain't', 'gonna', 'popples'); colourful/figurative expressions ('to boot', 'ha'); rhetorical questions/statements ('who'd have thought', 'no mistaking'); ellipses)

- Organise the class into groups to discuss Felicity in more depth by answering these questions: *What is your impression of Felicity? What gives you this impression? What other aspects to Felicity are revealed in the book?* (backpack containing amazing amounts to keep spirits up, for example, tea and cakes; tingling toes signalling something bad to come). *Are these in line with what you know of her?* (yes) *Would you like to meet Felicity? Why?* Hold a plenary to share ideas.

- By the end, the twins see Harriet and Felicity as family. Ask: *What role does Felicity play for the twins (and crew) as part of a family?* (nurturing, keeping spirits up, resourceful)

Differentiation

Support: Organise children in mixed ability groups to support each other.

Extension: Children can write two paragraphs describing Felicity's role as a character.

5. Character profiles

Objective
To draw inferences about characters.

What you need
Copies of *Brightstorm*, photocopiable page 30 'Character profiles'.

What to do
- Arthur and Maud are introduced in Chapter 1. Ask: *What clues suggest the twins are very close?* (good-natured bickering, knowing each other's thoughts, similar features, tying Maudie's ribbon together, Maudie's care over Arthur's arm, spending much time alone together)

- Discuss how Arthur and Maudie are very close but also very different. Explain that groups will re-read chapters to scan for detail on the twins (their situation and appearance, what they are like, and their talents and challenges). Also explain that this will help them to understand how the author builds their characters – sometimes describing (appearance), and sometimes allowing the reader to infer through dialogue, interests (for example, how the ship works or the library), props (like Maudie's toolbelt and Arthur's arm) and actions.

- Groups can choose one or more chapters to scan, or you can allocate chapters to groups, for example Chapters 4, 6, 10, 12, 13. Hand out copies of photocopiable page 30 'Character profiles' to the children to support them in building their character profiles.

- Bring the class together and read Chapter 6 from 'Remember what you started telling me...' to 'The last three Brightstorms against the world.' Ask groups to consider 'the bright light' inside Arthur and Maudie as 'Brightstorms' and to present a brief character profile of the twins based on their research. They should mention what the twins will never give up on and what special talents or skills will prove useful in the story.

- Later in the novel, revisit the twins' profiles, noting how they have changed or matured and what evidence supports this.

Differentiation
Support: Allocate groups specific chapters to re-read to focus on one twin.

Extension: Children can select chapters further on in the novel to see if their profiles and predictions ring true.

6. The case against Eudora Vane

Objective
To draw inferences and justify them with evidence.

What you need
Copies of *Brightstorm*.

Cross-curricular link
PSHE

What to do
- Re-read Chapter 19, asking the children to jump in at periodic intervals, appreciating the mood, vocabulary and figurative expressions. Ask: *What physical evidence suggests Eudora Vane was behind the* Aurora's *crash?* (marks on hydra-valve) *What does Arthur think caused them?* (sapient insect/ Eudora's brooch) *What confirms sabotage to the crew?* (Mr Smethwyck on Eudora's ship and Eudora gloating and asking for pitch)

- Ask: *If the case against Eudora went to court at this point, would she be convicted? Why?* (no; there is insufficient hard evidence; everyone believed her before, so Brightstorm name is not trustworthy) *What evidence do the twins collect?* (photographs of toxic plants and poison cake recipe, Eudora's locket, Arthur's journal noting site of *Violetta* and only 13 graves, Dad's diary) *What happens to this evidence?* (Eudora destroys it.) *What else do they find?* (Dad's camera) Finally, ask: *Why did Eudora do what she did?*

- Ask: *Is Dad's camera enough to convict Eudora Vane?* Organise groups to prepare a court case against Eudora Vane. Half of each group will prosecute Eudora (trying to prove she's guilty) and the rest will defend her. Explain that each side will make a speech to another group (jury) presenting the evidence for their side. The jury will then ask questions before deciding whether Eudora is guilty. Remind children that in a court of law, while evidence is needed to back up what is said, persuasive language and building a strong argument are also important, especially if there is a strong motive.

Differentiation
Support: Limit the evidence for some groups to use to build their arguments.

Extension: Groups can work on their persuasive speeches and present them to another class.

7. The twins' journey

Objective

To identify and discuss conventions in and across writing.

What you need

Copies of *Brightstorm*, photocopiable page 31 'The twins' journey'.

What to do

- Briefly recall the five-step classic story structure, writing the stages on the board (Introduction, Problem, Build-up, Climax, Resolution and Conclusion). Discuss the plot of *Brightstorm* with the children, matching events to the different stages.

- Now explain story structure as a journey. Many stories (traditional and modern) involve quests or journeys, either physical or personal journeys, with the protagonist(s) overcoming many challenges and returning changed or transformed. Briefly outline the common structure: the call (to action), the hero's companions, the journey, the helpers, arrival and frustration, final ordeals, the goal. Invite children to contribute examples from their own knowledge (for example, films) or reading (Hercules, *The Hobbit,* Percy Jackson, *Charlotte's Web,* Lyra Silvertongue, *Journey to the River Sea*).

- Hand out photocopiable page 31 'The twins' journey' and explain that pairs are going to map the twins' adventures in *Brightstorm* according to the journey structure, allocating chapters and events to the different stages in their 'journey'. Work though the first stage (the call: Chapters 1–6) together, to establish the context for the journey and the ultimate goal: to find out the truth about their father and clear the Brightstorm name.

- When children have finished, bring the class together and invite volunteer pairs to explain how the twins have changed (one twin each) or grown up by the end of their journey.

Differentiation

Support: Pairs can consider how just one of the twins has changed.

Extension: Children can summarise the key elements of the plot in terms of the journey structure. Encourage adverbials and other cohesion devices to link paragraphs smoothly.

8. Themes

Objective

To identify and discuss themes.

What you need

Copies of *Brightstorm*.

Cross-curricular link

PSHE

What to do

- Revise the difference between a book's plot (storyline) and its theme/s (main idea/messages). Themes in children's literature often deal with ways to cope with common dilemmas, fears and hopes children experience. Questions help identify themes; ask: *What challenges do the characters face? What do they learn?* Write common themes on the board, such as friendship, overcoming adversity, growing up or being different. Ask the children to describe themes they have encountered, supported with examples, from their independent reading.

- Organise the children into groups to answer the question: *What themes underlie this story?* (friendship, trust, resilience/perseverance, teamwork, justice, growing up, family, environmentalism, respect for each other and our differences) Hold a plenary to share their ideas using examples from the story, encouraging groups to build on each other's ideas while also listening respectfully. Write each theme on large card, backed by examples from the story. Survey the class to ascertain their view on the most important theme and why.

- Now broaden the discussion on themes to what we can learn from the story despite the different context, for example, understanding that everyone has their own talents or people should not be judged superficially on what they look like, who they are or where they come from. Following the discussion, ask: *Which characters do you identify with most and why?* Finally, ask the children to choose a theme from the board and write a paragraph explaining how it is reflected in the book.

Differentiation

Support: Provide the children with the evidence to support one of the themes to use in their paragraph.

Extension: Encourage the children to write about more than one theme.

Who am I?

- Use Chapters 7 and 8 to gather information about Felicity Wiggety and Harriet Culpepper, using these questions as a guide. Make notes in your book, using evidence from the text (record page numbers of relevant extracts).

General

1. How is she introduced?

2. What does she look like?

3. What does her personality seem like? Give examples.

Felicity

1. What has Felicity done in the past?

2. How does she react to Arthur's arm? Why doesn't he mind?

3. What jokes or puns does she make?

4. What kind gesture does she make to the twins?

5. What does the tingling in her toes mean?

6. Do you like her? Why?

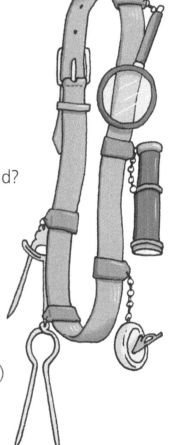

Harriet

1. What has Harriet done in the past? (see end of Chapter 6)

2. How does she react to Arthur's arm?

3. What suggests she is not always serious?

4. What is her dream?

5. What do you think she thinks of the twins?

6. What characteristics do you think she is looking for in possible crew members?

7. Do you like her? Why?

- Write down three questions you have about each character.

- Write down five adjectives to describe each character.

- Why do you think the twins like both characters?

Character profiles

- Use the profiler tool below to build your character profile. Draw your character in the middle based on descriptions and then surround the portrait with words and detail to build their profile. Include page references to relevant evidence/extracts.

Name:	Appearance:	Situation:
Age:		
Interests:	Portrait:	Talents:
Challenges:		What they think/worry about:

Your favourite thing about Arthur/Maudie and why:

The twins' journey

- Allocate chapters and events to the different stages in the twins' journey in the story.

The call to action – Chapters:
Key events:

The hero's companions – Chapters:
Key events:

The journey – Chapters:
Key events:

The helpers – Chapters:
Key events:

Arrival and frustration – Chapters:
Key events:

Final ordeals – Chapters:
Key events:

The goal – Chapters:
Key events:

TALK ABOUT IT ▶

1. Figuratively speaking

Objective
To build children's vocabulary.

What you need
Copies of *Brightstorm*, photocopiable page 35 'Figuratively speaking'.

What to do

- Write the words 'figurative' and 'literal' on the board. Ask: *Can you recall what these terms mean? What is a figure of speech and can you think of an example?* (A figurative expression uses words and phrases for effect, for example as 'cold as ice'; a literal expression uses words that mean exactly what they say, for example 'ice is cold'.) Share examples.

- Revise the meaning of figurative terms such as: simile (a comparison using like or as), metaphor (a direct comparison), personification (giving a non-living object human qualities), alliteration (repeated consonants), onomatopoeia (sounds), pun (a play on words that gives a word multiple meanings), oxymoron (a word or phrase that puts two opposing ideas together), idiomatic expression (a figurative phrase).

- Point out that the story has many examples of figurative language. Ask: *Why does the author use figurative language? What effect does it have?* Find examples from the text and discuss the effect.

- Hand out photocopiable page 35 'Figuratively speaking'. Invite the children to find examples in the story and then come together and share ideas. Prompt them to invent their own figurative language linked to the characters and the story.

- Encourage the children to keep the list going, possibly adding figurative expressions to the English working wall as they continue to read.

Differentiation
Support: Children revise the difference between figurative and literal. Support them with examples.

Extension: Children can make up their own examples of oxymorons in a range of categories, such as 'clothes: long shorts'.

2. An inventor's guide

Objective
To participate in presentations.

What you need
Copies of *Brightstorm*, Extract 4.

Cross-curricular link
History

What to do

- Begin by asking the children to name some famous inventors in history and their inventions (this is a good opportunity to test their general knowledge). Read aloud Extract 4 to remind the children of the people who invented floating balloons that could carry passengers.

- Inspired by real life, the story is filled with unique inventions. In small groups, ask the children to list some of them (Arthur's iron arm; a compass invented by Maudie; the *Aurora* – a sky-ship invented by Harriet Culpepper). Share ideas.

- Using the book cover, descriptions in the story and Extract 4, identify sky-ship features and criteria. Write them on the board: size, shape, fuel, manoeuvrability, materials, speed, safety.

- In small groups, invite the children to invent their own sky-ship. They should come up with a unique design, draw and label a sketch and add important information.

- Groups then prepare a presentation to explain each part of the ship and any challenges like the one mentioned in Chapter 22 ('No balloon can take the altitude').

- Groups take turns to present their invented sky-ship to the class and answer questions about it afterwards. The class can rate each ship on a scale of 1–5 according to the criteria discussed.

Differentiation
Support: Children work in groups, pairs or individually according to the support they require.

Extension: Draw up a table to compare all the sky-ships and transportation mentioned in the story.

3. Be persuasive

Objective
To use appropriate register. To articulate and justify arguments and opinions.

What you need
Copies of *Brightstorm*.

Cross-curricular link
PSHE

What to do

- Read Chapter 8 aloud from 'He stepped aside and gestured for them to enter' to 'The door closed', modelling fluency and expression. Ask: *Why did the children go to meet Harriet?* (They had applied to be part of her crew.) *How did they feel about meeting Harriet?* (nervous, eager, overwhelmed, desperate) *Why?* (They wanted to prove themselves worthy crew members; she was older and an experienced explorer – they were in awe.)

- Point out the persuasive tone and language in the dialogue. Ask: *What things do the children say they can do? What reasons do they give for being good candidates? What is their tone? Do you think they sound convincing? What did Harriet think?* Provide sentence stems to assist the discussion: 'The children want to convince Harriet that… because…'; 'They are determined to…'; 'Their tone is…'

- Working in pairs, invite the children to plan and prepare a persuasive speech for Arthur and Maudie, to convince Harriet to take them on her trip. The speech should include an introduction explaining who they are, a body with three good reasons and a conclusion summarising their proposal.

- Alternatively, children can work alone. They choose another scene such as in Chapter 9 where Eudora Vane tries to convince the children not to go, or Chapter 16 where Temur and Batzorig try to persuade them to stay. They prepare a persuasive speech by one of these characters.

Differentiation
Support: Rather than preparing a speech, children read aloud from the story focusing on a persuasive tone.

Extension: Children practise being persuasive in reversed roles: Harriet persuading the children to join her expedition.

4. A tight situation

Objective
To read aloud with fluency and understanding.

What you need
Copies of *Brightstorm*, Chapter 10.

What to do

- Turn to an extract in Chapter 10 from ''There's nothing,' Arthur called.' to 'Great, and we're a lot flatter.' Read aloud to the children, demonstrating fluency and expression. Ask: *Can you identify techniques used in the text, and in your reading, to express rising tension and panic?* (short, sharp sentences, repetition, capital letters, dashes and ellipses, exclamations, figurative language)

- Recall that the narrative explains *how* the characters behave and speak. Invite volunteers to explain what 'Arthur snapped' sounds like and to demonstrate 'He squinted at his sister'.

- Contrast the rising panic in the first part of the text, the ray of hope in the middle and the sense of relief at the end. Reflect on emotions, highlighting expressive words and phrases such as 'stuck fast', 'kicked the door', 'panic rising', 'light cut into the cellar', 'wood groaned', door creaked', 'one more mighty effort', 'wrench', 'ping', 'flung', 'crashing'.

- Children take turns to re-read the text to a partner using the strategies demonstrated, assisting each other, and highlighting areas for improvement or success.

- Focus on impact. Discuss how the sense of panic ends and is replaced by relief. Ask: *How does the author use humour to relieve the tension? Is it effective? Is it realistic in a situation of desperation to experience humour?* Provide sentence stems to help the children respond: 'In my opinion…'; 'In my experience…'; 'I have learned that…'; 'I think it's realistic because…'

Differentiation
Support: In groups, children re-read the text chorally, demonstrating expression and fluency.

Extension: In pairs, children choose another dialogue, then read it aloud, focusing on fluency and expression.

5. Standing out

Objective
To participate actively in collaborative conversations.

What you need
Copies of *Brightstorm*, photocopiable page 36 'Standing out'.

Cross-curricular link
PSHE

What to do

- Re-read the opening scene in the first chapter together. Ask: *What were the children doing in this scene? Did Arthur need help? Why? How did Maudie help him? What do you realise is special about his arm? What does Maudie mean by 'You totally had it, Arty'?*

- Consider the views of the other characters towards Arthur. Ask: How do others react to Arthur? (In Chapter 3, Mrs Beggins calls them 'unwanted scraps'; in Chapter 7, Felicity calls him 'harmless'; in Chapter 11, Mr Beggins describes Arthur as a 'good-for-nothing, broken boy'; in Chapter 28, Eudora calls him a 'half-formed boy'; in Chapter 12, the crew were kind, didn't stare or make awkward comments.) Discuss what their views suggest about their character. Provide sentence stems to assist the children in their responses: 'I think…'; 'In my opinion…'; 'Some would say…'; 'Their reactions show that they are…'

- Continue to analyse reactions. Ask: *Why does Maudie invent dramatic scenarios for why Arthur has a mechanical arm?* (trying to pre-empt people's thoughtless reactions that might hurt Arthur by making them see him as brave) *Do they all believe her? Why?* (Some do and some don't: those who don't believe her are the people who don't see anything 'wrong' with him.)

- In groups, children use photocopiable page 36 'Standing out' to discuss the topic further, then report back to the class.

Differentiation
Support: The children find and discuss examples where Arthur finds things challenging and times when his arm is useful.

Extension: The children talk about prejudice. Find examples in the story.

6. The Explorer's Code

Objective
To consider different points of view and build on the contributions of others.

What you need
Copies of *Brightstorm*, examples of explorers such as Ernest Shackleton, Edmund Hillary and Tenzing Norgay, photocopiable page 37 'The Explorer's Code'.

Cross-curricular links
PSHE, history, geography

What to do

- Write the word 'explorer' on the board. Ask: *What does an explorer do and where do they go? Do you know of an explorer?* Remind the children of some famous explorers in history. Share knowledge.

- Ask: *What do you think makes someone a good explorer?* Together, skim Chapter 6 and find examples of useful character traits and skills mentioned. Write them on the board.

- In Chapter 19, Harriet refers to 'The Explorer's Code'. Ask: *What is a code?* (a set of rules of behaviour for everyone to follow; standards of behaviour that define rights and wrongs) *Which part of the Explorer's Code does Harriet mention?* ('Assist fellow travellers first') *Do you think this is a good rule? Why?* Find other examples of expected behaviour (for example, Welby's advice in Chapter 10: 'Expedition relationships are based on trust'; Harriet's saying in Chapter 11: 'titles have no place here').

- In small groups, the children discuss and draw up the Explorer's Code using photocopiable page 37 'The Explorer's Code'. The code should include behaviour towards other explorers, the environment, animals and plants.

Differentiation
Support: Ask children to work in pairs and come up with one point per section.

Extension: The children use the Explorer's Code to compare Harriet and Eudora. They can find examples in the story like those in Chapter 17 to explain how Eudora Vane breaks the Explorer's Code.

Figuratively speaking

- Find examples from the story of figurative language.

Figurative language	Chapter	Example
Simile comparison using like or as		
Metaphor direct comparison		
Personification non-living object has human qualities		
Alliteration repeated consonants		
Onomatopoeia sounds		
Puns words with multiple meanings		
Oxymorons two opposite ideas together		
Idiomatic expressions figurative phrases		

- As you read the story, continue to add to these examples in this table or you can add them to the class working wall.
- Make up your own figurative language examples.

Standing out

- In groups, discuss and answer the following questions, giving your point of view and listening to other points of view. Make short notes below to help you.

1. In what way is Arthur physically different to others? Do you think he struggles to fit in?

_____

_____

_____

2. How do others treat him? Give examples.

_____

_____

_____

3. Does Maudie try to protect him? How?

_____

_____

4. How does Arthur's mechanical arm prove useful in the story?

_____

_____

5. How do you think it might feel to be Arthur and to be judged for being different?

_____

_____

6. Do you think people with physical challenges should be treated differently? Explain your answer and give examples.

_____

_____

The Explorer's Code

• Discuss rules that could be included in the Explorer's Code.

*I do solemnly swear to always abide by
the Explorer's Code in all circumstances.*

To my crew and fellow explorers, I will:

To the environment, I will:

To all animals and plants, I will:

GET WRITING ▶

1. The *Aurora* Report

> **Objective**
> To retrieve and record information. To use organisational and presentational devices.
>
> **What you need**
> Copies of *Brightstorm*, Extract 4, photocopiable page 41 'The *Aurora* report'.
>
> **Cross-curricular link**
> History

What to do

- Read Extract 4 together, pointing out the factual language and non-fiction features (headings, bullets, bold text, short sentences, timeline). Discuss the difference between fiction and non-fiction texts. Ask: *Can a fiction text contain facts? What is historical fiction/fantasy? What parts of this story – characters, places, objects – are based on facts? How does the author include factual language and information? What is the effect?* (It creates a realistic fantasy world where fantasy and reality mix.)

- In pairs, children take turns to read Chapter 12 to each other. Afterwards, write the following terms on the board and explain their meaning: port side, ship's deck, cog, wheel, sails, balloon.

- In groups, discuss the factual language used to describe the sky-ship *Aurora*. Invite the children to make notes under headings such as Physical features, Engine power, Modifications, Crew.

- Using photocopiable page 41 'The *Aurora* report', children create a non-fiction fact page on the *Aurora* using information from Chapter 12 and other references in the story. Children should aim to include non-fiction features such as those used in Extract 4. When they have finished, children can compare their fact sheets in groups.

> **Differentiation**
> **Support**: Children draw and label the *Aurora*.
>
> **Extension**: Children include a timeline of main events involving the *Aurora*.

2. Operation South Polaris

> **Objective**
> To note and develop ideas.
>
> **What you need**
> Copies of *Brightstorm*, photocopiable page 42 'Operation South Polaris'.
>
> **Cross-curricular link**
> Geography

What to do

- Begin by asking how the Brightstorm children felt about leaving home to find their father (nervous, unsure how to get there, not sure what to expect). Read the bit at the end of Chapter 4 where the children feel hopeless because 'We have no money, no ship, and that means no chance of going…' Ask: *How did their plan unfold?*

- Explain that the children should imagine they are setting up an expedition to South Polaris, and they must plan and prepare for it. Have a short class discussion on this scenario. Ask: *Who would you choose as your crew? What food and equipment are required?* Share ideas.

- In pairs, the children use a mind map to discuss ideas for their trip. They can design their own sky-ship and give it a name; they should also choose a crew based on skills and occupations required (see Chapter 12) and make a list of equipment needed (maybe including a tool belt like Maudie's). They should also think of a motto for the crew and even a logo for their ship.

- Using photocopiable page 42 'Operation South Polaris', the children work together to plan their expedition.

> **Differentiation**
> **Support**: The children explain the occupations mentioned in Chapter 12: meteorologist, botanist, engineer.
>
> **Extension**: The children create a digital slide show or poster with their information.

3. An explorer's journal

Objective

To identify the audience and purpose. To proofread for errors.

What you need

Copies of *Brightstorm*.

Cross-curricular link

PSHE

What to do

- Read Chapter 14 from 'Felicity poured the tea' to the end of the chapter. Ask: *What special book does Harriet give Arthur? What is the purpose? Why do you think she assigned this task to Arthur and not Maudie? Is it private or will someone else read it?*

- Later in the story, Arthur and Felicity discover their father's journal. Read Chapter 26 and then discuss the general features of a journal and specific things you might find in an explorer's journal. (General features: a date, first person narrative, factual descriptions, personal insights and perspective, colloquial language, usually past tense to describe past events but present tense to describe feelings and emotions. Specific features: daily temperature, co-ordinates, a map, observations, names of places and people, sketches of animals and plants with possibly a pressed leaf or flower as evidence.)

- Point out specific times when Arthur wrote in his journal and discuss what he might have written about (see Chapters 14, 15, 22, 25, 26). Ask: *Are there any other events that you think he might have recorded in his journal?*

- In groups, divide the task so that each child writes a journal entry for a different part of the expedition. Once they have planned it together, children write their section individually.

- Children work in groups again to edit and proofread each other's work.

Differentiation

Support: Prompt children to recall journal purpose, style and tone and write a personal journal entry.

Extension: Children create a daily schedule of tasks to be done on the sky-ship to add to the journal.

4. How to...make marsh cakes

Objective

To use organisational devices. To ensure consistent use of tense. To ensure correct subject and verb agreement.

What you need

Copies of *Brightstorm*, examples of recipes.

Cross-curricular links

Science, geography

What to do

- Encourage the children to talk about their favourite cakes and recipes. Ask: *Who likes to bake? Have you ever followed a recipe? Have you ever invented a recipe?* Look at actual recipes and discuss the language and features. Ask: *What common features do you find in recipes?* (title, list of ingredients and equipment needed, ordered instructions, command verbs, numbers or bullets, clear and precise language, present tense) Write them on the board, discussing and writing some common command verbs used in recipes (turn, mix, stir, add, combine, sieve, knead, grate, simmer, melt).

- At the beginning of Chapter 14, Felicity teaches Arthur to make marsh cakes. Ask: *What ingredients are mentioned? What ingredients are missing? What do they look like? What do they taste like? Do they sound good?*

- The children work in pairs to create their own recipe for marsh cakes (or any other edible items mentioned in the story – 'citadel cookies', 'Batzorig buns', 'home buns' or the 'deadly dessert'). They should begin with a diagram of their product, list the ingredients (real or imaginary), explain what to do using numbered steps, and include useful tips on how to cook them if there is no oven.

- Individually, the children write out the recipe paying attention to the features as listed above.

Differentiation

Support: Children revise the sentence structure of commands where the subject is missing (or implied) and the sentence begins with a verb. They also revise the use of the present tense.

Extension: Children write an explanation text on how to do something from the story ('How to build a shelter' or 'How to survive in snow') or giving directions ('How to get to South Polaris').

5. Thought-wolves

Objective
To select appropriate vocabulary. To describe characters.

What you need
Copies of *Brightstorm*, examples of kennings – traditional and modern.

What to do
- Read Chapter 20 together. Ask: *How would you describe the thought-wolves' way of speaking?* (mysterious, ancient, poetic, descriptive, literal, figurative) Identify words and phrases as examples.

- Write 'kenning' on the board. Explain that it is a type of figurative language associated with Old Norse-Icelandic poetry. Ask: *What do these ancient Viking kennings refer to: war-needles* (arrows), *sea-stallion* (ship), *earth-walker* (people), *battle-sweat* (blood), *sky-candle* (the sun), *ring-giver* (a king).

- Explain that a kenning is formed by two nouns, or a noun and a verb often joined with a hyphen. A kenning can be literal or figurative like these examples from the story: something that helps you find your way ('way-finder'), a wolf that uses thoughts to speak ('thought-wolf'), a floating vessel in the sky ('sky-ship', 'fire-bird'). Together, search Chapter 20 for other kennings.

- Model writing kennings on the *Aurora*. Brainstorm related nouns and verbs and try different combinations. Add adjectives, for example: 'sailing sky-vessel', 'cruising cloud-buster', 'powerful cog-turning giant'.

- In pairs, children invent kennings to suggest the way the 'thought-wolves' describe things.

Differentiation
Support: The children find kennings in the story (Arthur: 'crime solver'). Together, they write kennings to describe characters like Eudora Vane – for example, 'vile earth-walker' or 'evil two-legs', 'cruel insect-crusher'.

Extension: The children write kenning poems of 4 or 5 lines that include alliteration or assonance and other devices.

6. Read all about it!

Objective
To use devices to structure text. To build cohesion. To proofread for errors.

What you need
Copies of *Brightstorm*, photocopiable page 43 'Read all about it!'.

Cross-curricular link
Current affairs

What to do
- Together, skim the story to find various news reports and headlines (Chapters 2, 6, 30, 31). Ask: *What is each news article about? Who is involved? Is the news report always correct? How do you know?*

- Consider the headlines and ask the children if they remember the purpose of a news headline. Write the following words on the board and talk about how they are important in a news article: Who? What? Where? When? Why? How?

- In groups, children read the news articles in Chapters 30 and 31 in detail, paying attention to the style, tense and information included. For each article, identify the headline and answers to the questions on the board. Have a short report back.

- Remind the children that a news report usually provides the most important information first. Thereafter, the report includes less important information or detail with accounts from witnesses or hearsay from bystanders.

- Children then write a news report explaining the disappearance of Ermitage Wrigglesworth in Chapter 31 (introduced in Chapter 13). In pairs, children retrieve and gather information about him to plan the article using the question words to identify the key information. They should then use their imagination to come up with a news story. They then swap and proofread each other's work.

- The children use photocopiable page 43 'Read all about it!' to write the news reports out neatly for display.

Differentiation
Support: Use a writing frame (research 'the inverted pyramid') to guide children as they plan their report.

Extension: In groups, the children create a front and back page for their news report. They include other articles and advertisements.

The *Aurora* Report

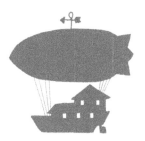

- Gather information about the *Aurora* and then write a fact page for the Geographical Society.

- Use the following headings and sections to record the data. In your description at the bottom make sure you use factual language, leaving out descriptive adjectives and opinions.

Diagram:	Captain and crew:
	Basic features:
Unique capabilities and modifications:	
Description:	

Operation South Polaris

- Plan an expedition to the South Polaris. Make notes below.

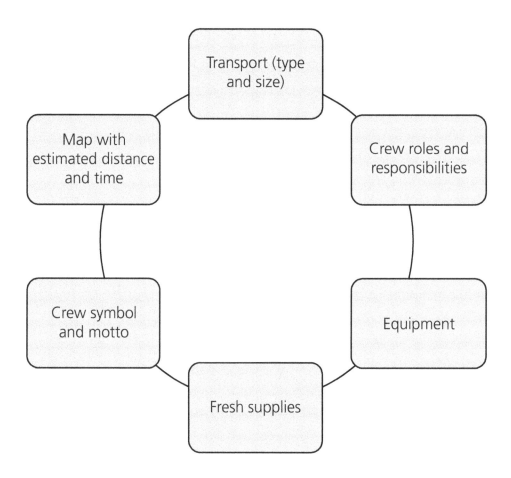

- Provide further details:
  - Draw and describe the crew symbol.
  - Draw your transport and add labels with explanations.
  - List the crew's occupations and explain their roles.
  - List the equipment and explain its purpose.

You may wish to use another sheet of paper to add all of the details above.

Read all about it!

- Write a news report explaining the disappearance of Ermitage Wrigglesworth.

- Include a headline in the box, a lead paragraph, other factual information and hearsay (or witness accounts) with some reported speech.

THE LONTOWN CHRONICLE

DATE:

ASSESSMENT ▶

1. Finish that thought...

Objective

To integrate dialogue to convey characters and their relationship.

What you need

Copies of *Brightstorm*, Extract 3.

Cross-curricular link

PSHE

What to do

- Read Extract 3 modelling fluency and expression. Ask: *What's happening in the dialogue between the characters?* (The twins are completing each other's sentences.)

- Take a closer look at how the dialogue is constructed. Ask the children to recall what they know about the use of ellipses (ellipses represent missing words, mark a pause, link ideas or indicate an incomplete thought) Ask: *What is the purpose of ellipses in this dialogue?* (links ideas) *What does this dialogue show about Arthur and Maudie's relationship?* (they're close; they understand each other and how they think and feel)

- In groups, invite the children to find other examples in the story of ellipses, particularly where the twins complete each other's sentences (see Chapters 1, 10, 17, 29).

- In pairs, invite the children to write a dialogue for a scene in the story where the characters complete each other's sentences. It could be the twins explaining what happened at the Geographical Society.

- The children write out their dialogue. They proofread and edit the dialogue. Then they read their dialogue aloud, demonstrating expression.

Differentiation

Extension: The children practise their dialogues then present them to other classes explaining the technique.

2. Questions in the Library

Objective

To demonstrate understanding of what they read and answer questions.

What you need

Copies of *Brightstorm*, Chapter 13, photocopiable page 47 'Questions in the library'.

What to do

- Explain that the children will complete a reading task by answering different types of questions. Revise question types and levels: lower-order questions require basic recall and yes/no/one-word responses; middle-order questions involve analysis of the text and classification; higher-order questions require opinion, interpretation and application of information based on the evidence provided. Provide examples to illustrate the different types of questions.

- Invite the children to recall tips for reading with understanding. Make notes on the board: first, skim the text for clues on what the text is about and the general context; second, read the text to gather details; third, read the questions to get an idea of the kind of information required; finally, scan the text again searching for specific information. Following these steps will prepare them to respond and express their understanding.

- Hand out copies of photocopiable page 47 'Questions in the library'. Give a reasonable time limit to allow the children to complete the activity on their own.

Differentiation

Support: Read the text together using choral or echo reading techniques to build confidence and comprehension. Allow extra time if necessary.

Extension: Add further higher-order questions to the ones provided.

3. One side of the story

Objective
To distinguish between the language of speech and writing and choose appropriate register. To proofread for errors.

What you need
Copies of *Brightstorm*.

Cross-curricular link
PSHE

What to do

- Begin by asking the children to recall the difference between first- and third-person narrative. (First-person narrative uses 'I' and gives reader insight into the character's thoughts and feelings and character is present in all scenes; third-person narrative uses 'he/she/they' and tells the story from an outsider's perspective.) Ask: *Can you recall examples of books told in different ways? Which do you prefer?*

- Ask: *Who narrates* Brightstorm*?* (third-person narrator) In pairs, find examples from the text. Ask: *What perspective does the narrator have? Is it different from the characters?* (The narrator tells the story from a third-person objective perspective – without knowledge of the future.) *Do you like the narrative style? Does it work well? Why?* Invite discussion.

- Together, read Eudora Vane's account of the failed expedition in Chapter 2 inviting children to jump in. Ask: *Who was Eudora speaking to? What is the effect of this first-person account?*

- Invite the children to retell an event of their choice from the perspective of a character in the story – it could even be Ernest Brightstorm giving his side of the story to the Geographical Society. They plot the events, making notes about what happened and how the character feels and thinks about it.

- Invite the children to draft their scene in first-person narrative, including the thoughts and feelings of the character who is telling the story. Afterwards children swap and proofread their work.

Differentiation
Support: Revise first- and third-person narrative with example sentences.

Extension: The children present the account as a speech for the Geographical Society.

4. Sapient animals

Objective
To gain, maintain and monitor the listeners' interest. To speak audibly and fluently.

What you need
Copies of *Brightstorm*, speech cards, Extract 4.

Cross-curricular links
Biology, geography

What to do

- In small groups, ask the children to list the sapient animals mentioned in the story (stoat, whales, Queenie the cat, Parthena the white hawk, the wolves, Miptera the silver insect, Altan – Batzorig's horse). Ask: *In what way are these animals different to our animals? What does sapient mean?*

- Discuss what the children know about these animals from the story. (Chapter 4 – loyal for life, rare in the Wide, usually only explorers could afford them). Ask: *How can information about these animals be organised?* (appearance, sapient characteristics, role in the story); write these headings on the board.

- In pairs, children research two sapient animals (Parthena and Miptera) and prepare a speech. They use the headings provided on the board, include examples from the story and a picture or diagram.

- Ask the children to recall presentation skills and ways to maintain audience interest (eye-contact, body language, levels of formality, expression, interesting and organised information, speech length and so on). Remind them to use speech cards with key words as prompts.

- Children practise and present their speeches to the class. Assess their speeches according to how clearly they speak and how they maintain the listeners' interest.

Differentiation
Support: Ask the children to make a poster of the sapient animals in the story to present to the class with headings, labels and snippets of information requiring less detail than the above activity.

Extension: Explain how the thought-wolves have evolved as sapient creatures and what makes them different. Children can create a poster or digital presentation to go with their speech.

5. A new beginning...

Objective

To write the beginning of the sequel in the same narrative style and tense. To predict what might happen from details stated and implied.

What you need

Copies of *Brightstorm*.

What to do

- Together, read the first and final chapter aloud, inviting readers to 'jump in' as directed. Ask: *How is the beginning different to the ending?* (The story begins with high-speed action that draws the reader in, but ends with a sense of calm and relief and also a mysterious clue as to what might follow.) Ask the children to briefly summarise what happens in the end (the Brightstorm family name is cleared, Eudora goes free, Ermitage Wrigglesworth goes missing) and to describe the tone (positive and mysterious). Ask: *How does the author create a sense that more is to come?* (the villain remains free, the children are ready for another adventure)

- Begin by reviewing the key features of *Brightstorm* and the historical fantasy fiction genre and then invite the children to imagine the beginning of the next adventure. Ask: *Will the sequel begin with another action scene? What will the children be doing? Who will they be with? Where will they be?* Discuss ideas. In small groups, children can plot events that might occur in the first chapter of the next book. Prompt them to include notes on the setting, characters, dialogue and plot.

- Individually, children plan and write the opening scene for the next story in the same narrative style and tense as the book. They should describe the setting, atmosphere and characters and include some dialogue.

- Afterwards, invite the children to read their opening scene aloud to the class.

Differentiation

Support: Children work together in pairs or small groups to draft and edit their text.

Extension: Children write more than just the opening scene – possibly a short chapter.

6. *Brightstorm* blurb

Objective

To summarise the story plot and review it. To use other writing as a model.

What you need

Copies of *Brightstorm*.

What to do

- Begin by asking: *Did you enjoy the book? What were your favourite parts? Who would you recommend it to? Does this story follow a traditional story structure?* (yes: it has a beginning, problem/challenge, build up, climax, conclusion/ resolution) *Can you recall similar stories you've read or watched or heard?* Invite responses.

- Read the blurb at the back of the book. Ask: *What is the purpose of the blurb and what information does the blurb provide?* (short summary, identifies main characters, gives general plot, identifies genre, gives clues as to what happens without giving the story away – contains no plot spoilers)

- Explain to the children that they will write their own blurb for *Brightstorm* to encourage others to read it. Using the existing blurb as a model, ask the children to recall the writing features and key elements of a blurb such as: identify the audience, use the third person, give some plot details in chronological order, use present tense, identify main characters, be concise.

- Individually, children write an extended blurb to promote *Brightstorm*. Provide sentence stems such as: 'The story is set in…', 'The main characters are…', 'The challenge they face is…', 'Things become exciting when…'. Remind them that the blurb can include some interesting plot details without giving away the ending.

- The children then check and edit their work.

Differentiation

Support: Summarise the plot on a timeline. Write interesting and useful vocabulary on the board.

Extension: The children write a review of *Brightstorm*. Provide a specific word count for the children to work towards.

 # Questions in the library

- Read Chapter 13 and then answer these questions in your book or on some paper.

- Answer the questions in your notebook.

1. How often did Arthur and Maudie visit the library?

2. What does the phrase 'sneaked off' imply?

3. Was the library filled with fiction or non-fiction books? Give some examples.

4. Why did the library 'feel like home' to Arthur?

5. Who was Ermitage Wrigglesworth?

6. Which book did Arthur find most interesting?

7. Give a synonym for the word 'lapped' and explain the effect of this word in the sentence: 'Arthur lapped up the details'.

8. What made the Acquafreedas interesting to Arthur?

9. What sentence shows that Maudie was not that interested in what Arthur was telling her?

10. What books did Maudie prefer to read? Why?

11. Why was Arthur's family not in the directory?

12. In what way did their father 'break the mould'?

13. What did Arthur discover about the Culpepper name?

14. What were the Vane family famous for?

15. Explain the expression: I can't put my finger on it.

16. What seemed strange to Arthur about the Vanes?

17. What is your favourite room? Describe it, giving some detail.

SCHOLASTIC
READ & RESPOND

Available in this series:

978-1407-15879-2

978-1407-14224-1

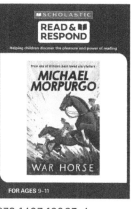
978-1407-16063-4

978-1407-16056-6

978-1407-14228-9

978-1407-16069-6

978-1407-16070-2

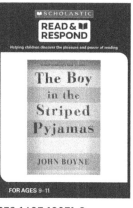
978-1407-16071-9

978-1407-14230-2

978-1407-16057-3

978-1407-16064-1

978-1407-14223-4

978-0702-30890-1

978-0702-30859-8

To find out more,
visit www.scholastic.co.uk/read-and-respond